Rugby Law

A Plain Language Guide

Rugby Law

A Plain Language Guide

Riley Bell
Mark Rowley

NEW ZEALAND
RUGBY UNION

REED

Published by Reed Books, a division of Reed Publishing (NZ) Ltd, 39 Rawene Rd, Birkenhead, Auckland. Associated companies, branches and representatives throughout the world.

ISBN 0 7900 0647 2

Edited by Peter Dowling
Illustrations by David Sheehan
Cover photograph: Andrew Cornaga/Photosport

First published 1998
Reprinted 1998
Revised edition published 1999
Printed in Australia

CONTENTS

FOREWORD

The New Zealand Rugby Football Union wishes to ensure that New Zealand rugby is viewed as the best in the world. As part of its efforts towards achieving that goal, the NZRFU is continually striving to create a domestic playing environment that features fair play and safe practices according to the laws of the game.

One of the NZRFU Referee Development Unit's primary objectives is to assist everyone associated with rugby in gaining a better appreciation of the laws of the game and the referee's role and contribution.

The introduction of *Rugby Law: A Plain Language Guide* to the retail market in 1998 represented a significant promotion of the laws of the game to the general rugby public in a style that is eminently readable and easily understood. It takes into account all of the Domestic Safety Law Variations applicable to New Zealand domestic rugby.

This guide will also continue to be used nationwide as a primary training resource for new referee recruits and referees in the early stages of their careers.

The NZRFU is indebted to the valuable input from Riley Bell and Mark Rowley who have been involved since its first publication in 1989.

I trust that this guide will assist you in coaching, playing, refereeing and viewing our national game. A greater understanding of the laws of the game will result in significantly more enjoyment for everyone concerned.

Rob Fisher
Chairman
New Zealand Rugby Football Union

PREFACE

Rugby Law: A Plain Language Guide sets out to make the laws of rugby available in an easily comprehensible form to rugby players and supporters at every level of the game in New Zealand.

The book was first written in 1989 to help coaches and players in all grades of rugby, particularly below Senior A, become better acquainted with the laws of the game. Since that time it has been adopted by the NZRFU as a standard training resource and has been regularly updated as the IRB laws have changed.

Coaches and players in senior rugby should already be thoroughly familiar with the full laws of the game. It must be emphasised that this book is not intended as a substitute for that publication. Many technical points have been omitted, especially as they relate to refereeing, as have some laws applying to less common situations.

Realistically, we know that many players, coaches and fans will, for various reasons, never read the full version of the laws. So this book tries to simplify the phrasing and layout of the laws without at the same time oversimplifying them.

A general familiarity with the main features of the game is assumed, so some more obvious definitions and laws have been omitted. In places, the laws have been explained in more detail than in the original, or comment has been added where, as referees, we have noted players and coaches having trouble with a particular aspect of play.

This book is not definitive, it does not cover all situations and should not be solely relied on by parents, teachers or coaches when they have to take up a whistle in the absence of a union-appointed referee. But we hope it makes the laws rather more easy to understand and enables coaches, players and all followers of the game better to appreciate the referee's task. As familiarity and understanding of the laws increase, so does enjoyment.

The laws are correct as at 1 March 1999 and incorporate both the International Law and the New Zealand Domestic Safety Law Variations. Where the international and domestic laws vary, the differences are clearly stated. Variations in scrum law are the most notable, with the Domestic Safety Law Variations applying to games below Senior A level. Further variations occur in player numbers between different levels of domestic rugby and games in the Super 12 competition or with visiting overseas sides.

In large part, the sequence and wording of the section headings follow those of the laws themselves as given in the NZRFU manual *Laws of the Game*. The actual law covered is noted at the start of each section.

Riley Bell
Mark Rowley
North Harbour Rugby Referees Association

Riley Bell and Mark Rowley have more than 30 years refereeing experience between them as members of the North Harbour Rugby Referees Association. The pair have been involved in rugby law tuition and instruction to referees at provincial level for many years. Riley Bell has lectured on rugby law at national level for more than a decade, and has been a member of the NZRFU Laws Advisory Group since 1991.

I. THE GROUND

The playing area consists of the field-of-play and the in-goal area.

The field-of-play is bounded by the touch-lines and goal lines, but does not include them. The touch-line is in touch, and the goal line is in in-goal.

Each in-goal area is bounded by the goal line, the touch-in-goal lines and the dead-ball line but does not include the touch-in-goal lines, nor the dead-ball line, nor the corner posts which are part of touch-in-goal. The goal posts are in the in-goal area (see section 10, In-Goal).

Thus it is possible to score a try on the goal line and for the ball to be dead on the dead-ball line.

The 22 metre lines are part of the 22 metre area.

The playing enclosure is the playing area and a reasonable area surrounding it, and is under the control of the referee. It should be noted that reserves and coaches do not have a right in law to be on the sideline or in the playing enclosure.

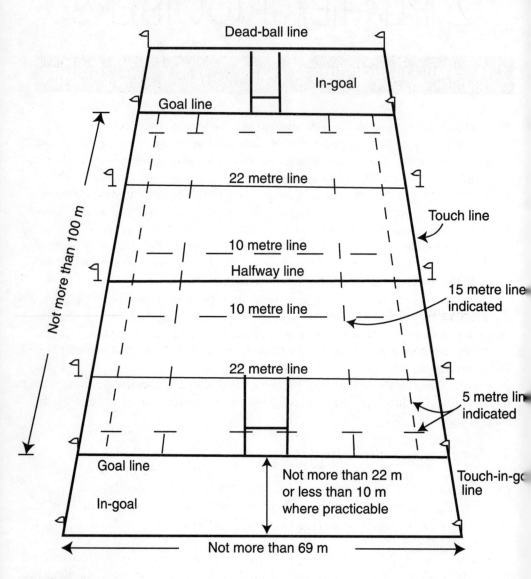

Dead-ball line

In-goal

Goal line

Not more than 100 m

22 metre line

Touch line

10 metre line

Halfway line

15 metre line indicated

10 metre line

22 metre line

5 metre line indicated

Goal line

Not more than 22 m or less than 10 m where practicable

In-goal

Touch-in-goal line

Not more than 69 m

The field of play.

2. PLAYER NUMBERS

- At all levels of New Zealand rugby, team squad size may be up to a maximum of 22 players.
- If the official squad consists of 22 players, five of the players must be qualified and trained to play in the front row.
- For squads of 21 there must be four players qualified and trained to play in the front row.
- For squads of 20 or less there is no requirement specifically to nominate front row reserves.
- If a team cannot provide three qualified and trained front row players prior to the match commencing then they forfeit the match.

1. Permanent Replacements

At all levels of New Zealand rugby, seven players may be substituted or replaced for injury, but once a player has been replaced for an injury he cannot resume playing in the match.

If on medical advice or for any other reason the referee considers it would be harmful for an injured player to continue playing, a player may be required to leave the playing area.

2. Temporary Replacements

Any player who has an open or bleeding wound must leave the field of play, until such time as the bleeding is controlled and the wound is covered or dressed.

When this occurs a temporary replacement player may come onto the field of play. If the injured player does not return then the temporary replacement becomes permanent.

The same rules apply for other injuries except that the temporary replacement is limited to ten minutes, but unlike the open or bleeding wound it is not mandatory for those players to go to the sideline for treatment.

When temporarily replacing an injured player the following rules apply:
- The ball must be dead.
- The referee must be informed and approve.
- Where a reserve touch judge has been appointed to the match then the control of the replacements and substitutes lies with him.

Any breach of the substitute/replacement rules will result in a penalty kick.

3. Substitutions

All teams may make up to seven tactical substitutions or injury replacements during the match. This in effect means that a team may have 22 players in it, of which 15 are on the field of play at any one time.

Players who have been substituted and are not injured may replace an injured player, but may not otherwise play again.

However, when a substitution is made the following rules apply:
- The substitution can only be made when the ball is dead.
- The referee must be informed of, and approve, the substitution.

4. Players Ordered Off or Temporarily Suspended

At all levels of domestic rugby in New Zealand, any player ordered off or placed in the sin bin under the foul play provisions (see section 10, Foul Play) cannot be replaced with the following exception.

Exception

If a front row player should be ordered off or sin binned he may be replaced, but in this case the captain of that team will have to reduce his team to 14 players by requiring another forward to leave the field of play.

The following table may help clarify the laws on these matters.

NEW ZEALAND DOMESTIC RUGBY - ALL LEVELS
Law 3: Number of Players

Number in Squad	Front Row Players	Max. Substitutes/Replacements
20 or less	3	Max. 5
21	4	Max. 6
22 (Max.)	5	Max. 7

In summary:

1. An injured player, once permanently replaced, cannot resume playing.

2. Blood bin injuries may have a temporary replacement player.

3. Blood bin injuries have no time limit.

4. Non blood bin injuries: These players are permitted to be temporarily replaced for up to a maximum of ten minutes. After ten minutes the temporary replacement becomes a permanent replacement.

5. Substituted players are permitted to be used as temporary or permanent replacements.

TEST MATCHES, WORLD CUP, TRI-NATIONS AND SUPER 12

- It is not permitted to replace injured players temporarily.
- If the official squad consists of 16, 17 or 18 players, at least four of the players must be qualified and trained to play in the front row.
- For squads of 19, 20, 21 or 22 players, at least five of the players must be trained and qualified to play in the front row.
- Only two front row players and five other players may be substituted.
- Substituted players may be used to replace an injured front row player only if no other suitably trained replacement is available; otherwise they are not permitted to take the field again.
- If a front row player is ordered off and there is a reserve front row player available to take his position, the referee will require the captain to nominate another forward to leave the playing area, and the reserve player may then replace the dismissed player.

   If the only front row player available has been substituted off earlier in the match, then he may be utilised under these special circumstances.
- Where there is no suitable replacement, the game will continue with 'Golden Oldies' scrums (see page 47).

CONCUSSION

Coaches should particularly note that a player who has suffered concussion must not participate in any match or training session for a period of at least three weeks from the time of injury, and then only subject to being cleared by a proper neurological examination.

3. DRESS

Players must not wear dangerous projections such as buckles, rings, earrings or pendants. A referee may inspect players' dress before or during a match and require sharp or otherwise unacceptable studs, and dangerous items, to be removed or rectified and only then permit the player concerned to resume playing.

Headgear must be primarily designed to protect the ears or the head against abrasion from hard grounds and must not be thicker than 1 cm when uncompressed. It must be understood that medical advice indicates that headgear provides no protection against concussion.

Shoulder pads of the harness (or league) type must not be worn. Shoulder pads that cover only the shoulders and collar bone and are no thicker than 1 cm when uncompressed are acceptable. They must not have a sternum plate or reinforcing across the chest with the exception that women may have a chest pad built into their padding.

All players in New Zealand domestic rugby are now required to wear mouth guards during the match.

A player may not wear:

- shoulder pads of the harness type.
- braces or supports which include any rigid or reinforced material.
- protective garments on any part of the body, except as above.
- helmets or head guards, except as above.
- clothing which has become bloodstained during the match.
- gloves.
- dangerous projections such as buckles or rings.

Studs
Maximum length to sole: 18 mm.
Minimum diameter at tip: 10 mm.

The wearing of a single stud at the toe is prohibited. The moulded multi-studded sole is acceptable, as are the rubber-soled boots known as 'blades'.

It should be noted that the law requires a player who has had his gear inspected prior to the match and is then found to be wearing prohibited items during the game to be ordered off.

When part of a player's dress or gear has blood on it, depending on the circumstances, the referee must require the gear to be replaced before carrying on with the game (see section 2, Player Numbers).

TEST MATCHES, WORLD CUP, TRI-NATIONS AND SUPER 12

There is no requirement for players to wear mouthguards.

4. TIME

The duration of play shall be as directed by the union, or, in the absence of such direction, as agreed upon by the teams, or if not agreed, as fixed by the referee.

The interval shall be up to a maximum of ten minutes and players may now leave the field of play for that period. Most provincial unions limit the interval to five minutes for club matches and referees should check with the parent union on local policy.

Normally, no more than one minute shall be allowed for injury treatment.

Playing time lost in excess of 40 seconds for a kick at goal shall be added, as shall injury time, to that half of the match in which it occurred. Also, time needed for replacing or substituting players should be added on.

If time expires after a set piece (e.g. scrum, line-out) has been awarded but before it has commenced, the referee will permit the completion of that phase until the ball next becomes dead before ending the match.

TEST MATCHES, WORLD CUP, TRI-NATIONS AND SUPER 12

All matches are of two 40-minute halves, with the ability to play extra time for pool matches requiring elimination of teams in knock-out competitions (see section 24, Tournament Rules).

5. THE REFEREE AND TOUCH JUDGES

The Referee

The referee shall be appointed by the union; if not, then as mutually agreed between the teams; failing any agreement, he shall be appointed by the home team.

If the referee is unable to complete the match he may appoint a replacement or, if he is unable to do so, the home team shall appoint a replacement.

The referee keeps the time and the score. He has the power to end the game before time has expired if in his opinion the full time cannot for any reason be played or continuation of play would be dangerous.

The referee is the sole judge of fact and law. All his decisions are binding on the players. He may not alter a decision except in a few special cases such as subsequently seeing that a touch judge's flag is raised.

All players must stop playing at once when the whistle blows. All players must respect the authority of the referee and they must not dispute his decisions. Failure to do so will be penalised as misconduct, and could result in a player being ordered off.

A player must not leave the playing enclosure without the referee's permission. If a player retires during a match because of injury or otherwise, he must not resume playing until the referee or reserve touch judge has given permission.

The Touch Judges

If none have been appointed by the union, each team shall provide a touch judge. He is under the control of the referee who may instruct him on his duties and may overrule any of his decisions.

The touch judge must hold up his flag when the ball or a player carrying it has gone into touch and must indicate the place of throw-in and which team throws in. The touch judge must keep his flag raised:

1. When the thrower puts any part of either foot in the field-of-play.

2. When the ball has been thrown in by the wrong team.

3. When, at a quick throw-in, the ball that went into touch is not used, or after going into touch, the ball has been touched by someone other than the player throwing it in.

It is for the referee to decide whether the ball has been thrown in from the correct place.

Reserve touch judges are given delegated authority by the match referee to control the players coming onto the field of play either as substitutes or replacements. Players who do not comply with the reserve touch judge's directions will be penalised and may be ordered off.

6. ADVANTAGE

Laws 8 and 9

The referee shall not whistle for an infringement during play which, in the referee's judgement, is followed by an advantage to the other team. The referee has a wide discretion in applying advantage, and it should be noted that the advantage is not limited to teritorial gains. Teams should play to the whistle after an apparent infringement, whether or not the referee calls or signals advantage. This is true for a wide range of infringements from a knock-on to a serious offence. In fact, outside of immediately dangerous situations, there are only three occasions when advantage will not be played:

1. When the ball or ball carrier touches the referee in the field-of-play, play shall continue unless the referee considers either team has gained an advantage, in which case he shall order a scrum; put-in to the team that last played the ball.

2. When the ball emerges from either end of the scrum tunnel without having first been played (i.e. touched) by a front row player.

3. In the accidental off-side situation, play should be allowed to continue unless the infringing team gets an advantage, in which case a scrum shall be formed at that place.

It should be noted that some laws require the referee to apply advantage only if it occurs very quickly. Examples of this are to be found in the tackle law, the foul play law as it applies to dangerous tackles, and the collapsed scrum situation where the safety of players is paramount.

7. KICK-OFF

A kick-off starts play for each half and restarts play after a try or goal is scored.

1. A place kick is used to start the match and the second half. It must be taken from the centre of halfway.

    A drop kick is taken after the other team has scored and must be taken at or behind the centre of halfway. If taken from the wrong place or with the wrong type of kick it shall be kicked off again.

2. The ball must reach the opponents' 10 metre line. If it does not, then either it must be kicked off again or a scrum must be formed at the centre of halfway, at the opponents' option.

    However, if an opponent plays the ball before it reaches the 10 metre line play will continue.

    A mark cannot be awarded from a kick-off.

3. If the ball goes into touch on the full, the opponents may accept the kick (by opting for a line-out at halfway), or allow another kick, or take a scrum at the centre of halfway.

4. If at a kick-off the ball crosses the goal line without touching — or being touched by — a player, the defenders may either ground the ball, pick it up and play on, or make it dead by kicking it into touch-in-goal or over the dead-ball line. If they do ground the ball, or if it goes into touch-in-goal, or over the dead-ball line, they will get the option of another kick-off or a scrum at halfway.

    However, the options available under this law must be exercised without delay. Receivers cannot wait until an opponent arrives before taking one of the options. Neither can they pick up the ball and then run or pass it. If this occurs then they have 'played on' and the kick-off law is complete.

5. The kicker's team must be behind the ball when kicked, otherwise a scrum shall be formed at the centre of halfway.

6. The opposing team must stand on or behind the 10 metre line. If they are in front of that line or if they charge before the ball has been kicked, it shall be kicked off again.

8. TRY AND TOUCH-DOWN

Law 12

A clear understanding of grounding the ball is important. A player grounds the ball in the in-goal area by pushing the ball to the ground with hand or arm, even for an instant, or forcing it on the ground with the front of the body from waist to neck inclusive.

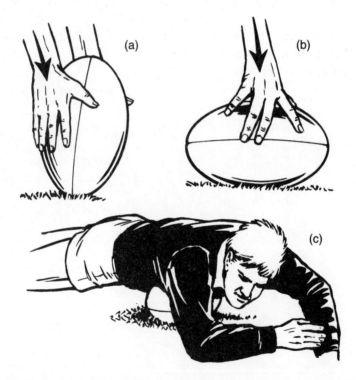

Grounding the ball: (a) pushing the ball to the ground, (b) applying downward pressure, (c) forcing it with the body.

A try is scored when a player who is in his opponents' in-goal first grounds the ball there.

A penalty try shall be awarded under the posts if foul play or off-side by the defending team prevents either:

1. A probable try being scored; or
2. The try being scored in a better position than where the ball was grounded.

The conversion is taken as usual.

Note that foul play covers many situations and can be interpreted very broadly. For instance, a breach of the tackled ball law by a defender near his goal line by failing to release the ball and rolling away could deprive an attacker of the ball and a try. This could be ruled as a deliberate infringement and may result in a penalty try being awarded.

A touch-down occurs when a player first grounds the ball in his own in-goal area. Play then restarts with either a drop-out or a 5 metre scrum as outlined in section 10, In-Goal.

9. CONVERSION

The kick at goal after a try may be by either a drop kick or a place kick. The defenders must be behind the goal line until the kicker begins his run or offers to kick, when they may charge or jump to prevent the goal.

For an early charge, shouting or similar misconduct by the defenders, and where no goal is scored, another kick shall be allowed without the charge.

If the ball rolls over before the kicker starts to kick, he should check with the referee before placing the ball. If the ball rolls over after the kicker has commenced his approach, then he must continue.

The kick shall be taken with the ball that was grounded for the try.

Kicking tees are mandatory at all levels of New Zealand rugby (but not Super 12) for all kicks at goal.

10. IN-GOAL

1. 5 Metre Scrum

A 5 metre scrum can be set from a variety of situations.

(a) Where there is doubt about which team first grounded the ball, or where a player with the ball is held in in-goal and cannot ground the ball, the scrum is set opposite that place and 5 m from the goal line (but no closer than 5 m to the touch-line).

(b) Where a defender carries the ball back, even if forced, or sends the ball back over the goal line and it there becomes dead (e.g. touchdown, into touch-in-goal or over the dead-ball lines) the scrum is set opposite the place where the ball became dead.

2. In-Goal Infringements

(a) If an attacker knocks on or passes forward in the in-goal or in the field-of-play but less than 5 m from the goal line and the ball travels into the in-goal area, and is then grounded by either team or goes into touch-in-goal or over the dead-ball line, a scrum is formed 5 m out, opposite the place of infringement, defenders' ball.

(b) If a defender knocks on or passes forward within his in-goal area and the ball is then grounded by a defender, or it goes into touch-in-goal or over the dead-ball line, a scrum is formed 5 m out, opposite the place of infringement, attackers' ball.

(c) (i) A penalty try should be awarded when by foul play in in-goal a defender prevents a probable try or its being scored in a better position.

(ii) A try should be disallowed and a penalty kick awarded 5 m from the goal line opposite the place of infringement if a try would probably not have been scored but for foul play by an attacker. Where a penalty kick has been awarded to the defenders after the ball has become dead but before the drop-out has been taken, the kick is to be taken anywhere along the 22, i.e. where play would have restarted but for the foul play. The same reasoning will apply for a penalty kick to the non-offending team to restart play at halfway after foul play following the awarding of a try.

(iii) For other offences in in-goal the outcome is the same as for in the field-of-play but the kick or scrum is awarded 5 m from the goal line opposite the place of infringement.

3. Drop-Out

If an attacker kicks or carries the ball into his opponents' in-goal and it is then grounded by a defender or else goes into touch-in-goal or over the dead-ball line, a drop-out is awarded.

4. Touch-in-Goal

This occurs when the ball or a player carrying it touches a corner post or a touch-in-goal line or the ground beyond it. So, where a defender with the ball is forced back from the field-of-play onto the corner post, a 5 metre scrum results. Where an attacker hits the corner post before grounding the ball, a drop-out results.

5. Rucks, Mauls, and Scrums

These end when the ball within them is on or over the goal line. The ball can be immediately grounded by any player, thus scoring a try or forcing a drop-out 22. If it is not grounded then it becomes 'held ball in goal' and a 5 metre scrum is awarded.

 Under New Zealand Domestic Safety Law the scrum is not allowed to be set closer than 5 m to the goal line and must be reset if it has moved more than 1.5 m. Thus, no 'push-over' tries are possible below club Senior A grades.

11. DROP-OUT

Law 15

A drop-out is a drop kick awarded to the defending team.

1. If a team kicks the ball over the opponents' dead-ball line or touch-in-goal line, either directly or after it bounces in the in-goal area, then the defending team may take the drop-out 22 or have the option of taking a scrum back at the place from where the ball was kicked.

   The exception to this law is when the attacking team has a genuine drop kick or penalty kick at goal that ultimately goes dead. The scrum option is not available in this circumstance.

2. The drop kick may be taken from anywhere on or behind the 22 metre line and must be taken without delay. If taken beyond the 22 metre line it must be dropped out again.

3. The ball must cross the 22 metre line — otherwise the opposing team may opt for another kick or for a scrum at the centre of the 22.

4. If the ball goes out on the full the opposing team may opt to accept the kick (by taking the line-out), or allow another drop-out, or have a scrum at the centre of the 22.

5. The kicker's team must be behind the ball when kicked, otherwise a scrum is taken at the centre of the 22. However, the kick may be taken quickly with the kicker's team in front of the ball. In this case these players are off-side and must retire until they are put on-side by their own team in accordance with law 25, on-side (see section 21).

6. The opposing team must not charge over the line, otherwise the ball shall be dropped out again. But, if an opposing player remains in the 22 metre area or crosses into it for the purpose of delaying or interfering with the kicker, a

penalty for misconduct should be awarded. If the kick had not yet been taken, the penalty spot would be at any place chosen on the 22.

The advantage law may be applied in all of the above situations including the ball failing to reach the 22 metre line.

12. FAIR-CATCH ('MARK')

A player makes a fair-catch, and is awarded a free kick, when he is within his own 22 metre area, or in-goal, and he cleanly catches the ball directly from a kick by one of his opponents and at the same time calls 'Mark!' The receiver may leap for the ball and he does not have to be on the ground as he makes the catch.

If he is in the air at the time of calling 'Mark!' then the place of the mark is where he claimed the mark, regardless of whether he lands in touch or outside the 22 metre area. A mark cannot be awarded from a kickoff.

The catcher must take the subsequent free kick himself.

It is dangerous play to tackle a player while he is in the air. Referees will invariably penalise players who do this.

13. KNOCK-ON AND THROW-FORWARD

A knock-on will only result in a scrum if the ball, after it has been knocked on by the arm or hand, actually touches the ground or another player (i.e. it has not been 'recovered' by the player as the law requires).

Knock-on: the ball must come only from a hand or arm and touch the ground or another player.

Frequently the ball may go to ground and bounce forward, or it may come off a player's chest or other than from a hand or arm, or a player may charge down a kick by an opponent. These situations are not knock-ons as defined in law and play will continue.

A knocked-on ball fly-kicked before touching the ground is not considered 'recovered', and this is an infringement.

A throw-forward occurs when a player carrying the ball throws, passes or hands it forward.

These infringements result in a scrum, normally at the place of infringement. An intentional throw-forward or knock-on results in a penalty kick.

Referees are instructed not to judge a knock-on or pass as an infringement unless clearly so. If there is any doubt, play should be allowed to continue.

These two infringements account for most applications of the advantage law. Players should continue playing until the whistle blows.

14. PENALTY KICK

Law 27

The Kicker's Team

1. The kick cannot be taken before the referee has made the mark. If this should occur play is null and void and the referee will bring the play back and require the kick to be taken again, on or directly behind the mark.

2. The kicker's team must be behind the ball for the kick. However, this does not prevent the kick being taken quickly. If this should occur the kicker's teammates who are in front of the kicker must be in the act of retiring and not loitering. They must keep retiring until they are on-side (see section 21, Off-Side and On-Side in General Play).

3. The kick must be taken with the ball that was in play and it must be with the foot or lower leg, and not the knee or heel. It must be taken without undue delay.

4. The kicker may kick the ball in any direction, but if holding the ball he must propel it out of his hands. If the ball is on the ground he is not permitted to keep his hand on it and must propel it a visible distance from the mark. In either case, a mere touch with the foot is not sufficient.

5. Any type of kick may be used, except that a player kicking for touch may use only a punt or drop kick. Once a kick at goal is indicated by a kicker he must then kick at goal. A scrum may be taken instead of a penalty kick if the team wishes.

6. If the place where the penalty would be awarded to an attacking team is within 5 m of the opponents' goal line, the mark for the kick shall be 5 m from the goal line. A defending team can be awarded a penalty within 1 m of its own goal line.

Infringement of any of the above results in a scrum at the mark, opponents' ball.

The Offending Team

1. The opposing team must run without delay (and continue to do so while the kick is being taken and while the ball is being played by the kicker's team) to, or behind, a line parallel to the goal lines and 10 m from the mark, or to their own goal line if that is less than 10 m from the mark.

2. If a kick at goal is taken they must remain quiet, passive and motionless with their hands by their sides until the kick has been taken.

3. If the kick is taken quickly, and the opponents are within 10 m of the mark, they must keep retiring and not obstruct the ball carrier. They may only enter the game after they have retired 10 m back from the mark itself or a team-mate who was the required 10 m back runs in front of them (see illustration, page 34). There are no actions that the opponents can take that will let them re-enter the game.

4. The opposing team must not prevent or delay the kick or interfere with the kicker in any way, nor wilfully interfere with the ball.

Infringement of any of the above will result in a penalty a further 10 m in front of the original mark. (See also section 22, Foul Play, for foul play offences before the kick is taken.) In this regard, backchatting the referee will almost certainly result in being marched a further 10 m downfield and, if by the kicker's team, a reversal of the penalty to the other team.

Where a penalty kick or free kick is taken before the referee has made a mark, including the case where a consequential kick is awarded, all subsequent play is null and void (including any 'try' that may have been 'scored'). The referee must bring the play back to the mark and require the kick to be taken when and where the mark is made.

15. FREE KICK

A free kick is awarded for a fair-catch and for various offences, especially relating to scrums and line-outs, generally of a technical nature.

A free kick can not be kicked into touch on the full if taken outside the 22 metre area. If this occurs the line-out will be taken from opposite the place where it was kicked.

A free kick to the attacking team may not be awarded closer than 5 m from the defending team's goal line.

The requirements for both teams are the same as for a penalty kick, except:

1. A goal can not be scored either directly or indirectly from a free kick. The team awarded a free kick may not score a dropped goal until after the ball next becomes dead or the ball has been played or touched by an opposing player.

 It should be noted that under this provision a free kick immediately followed by a maul or ruck satisfies the requirement of the opposing player 'playing or touching' the ball. If the kicking team should then win possession of the ball from this ruck or maul and successfully drop kick for goal, the referee would award the dropped goal notwithstanding the fact that the opponents may not have physically touched the ball in the ruck or maul.

2. Having first properly retired, opponents may charge to try to prevent the kick as soon as the kicker begins his run or makes any movement to kick.

3. If, having charged fairly, opponents prevent the kick from being taken, it is void, and a scrummage is set on the mark, charging team's ball.

4. If opponents lawfully charge down a free kick, once kicked, in the playing area, play should be allowed to continue.

Kick can not
be taken until
mark has been
made by referee.

Kick must be taken
at or behind a line
through the mark.

If a quick kick
is taken, opponents
must retire until 10 m
back from mark or
until another player
(e.g. No.11) moves forward
and puts them back into
the game.

Opponents
must retire
10 m.

10 m

Free kick and penalty kick.

5. If, from a free kick taken in the in-goal area, the ball travels into touch-in-goal or over the dead-ball line, or if the kick is void or incorrectly taken, the resulting scrum shall be 5 m from the goal line on a line through the mark, attackers' ball.

The kicker's team must be behind the ball for the kick. However, this does not prevent the free kick from being taken quickly. If this should occur the kicker's team-mates who are in front of the kicker must be in the act of retiring and not loitering. They must keep retiring until they are on-side (see section 21, Off-Side and On-Side in General Play).

As in the penalty kick situation, if the kick is taken quickly and the opponents are within 10 m of the mark, they must keep retiring and not obstruct the ball carrier. They may only enter the game after they have retired 10 m back from the mark itself or a team-mate who was the required 10 m back runs in front of them (see illustration, page 34). There are no actions that the opponents can take that will allow them to re-enter the game.

For an infringement by the kicker's team, apart from that outlined in paragraph 5 above, a scrum is given at the mark, non-kickers' ball. For an infringement by the opposing team, a free kick is given 10 m in front of the original mark.

Where a penalty kick or free kick is taken before the referee has made a mark, including any consequential kicks, all subsequent play is null and void (including any 'try' that may have been 'scored'). The referee must bring the play back to the mark and require it to be taken when and where the mark is made.

In all other respects, the free kick laws are the same as those for the penalty kick.

16. TACKLE, AND LYING WITH, ON OR NEAR THE BALL

It is vital that players understand the tackle law as it is fundamental to the character of the game. It is also a fact that the majority of penalties awarded in the game today result from breaches of this law.

The aim of the law is simply to give the tackled player a chance to keep the game flowing and thus provide the continuity to the game that makes it the spectacle that it can be.

Player tackled: passing ball

Player tackled: placing ball

Player not tackled: pushing ball away, arriving opponents must not dive on him

Options for a player who is tackled or goes to ground.

By definition, a tackle can occur only in the field-of-play, not in-goal. It occurs when a player with the ball is held by an opponent and, while held, the player has any other part of his body other than his feet on the ground or on another player lying on the ground. Thus two elements are required for a tackle to occur. Firstly, the ball carrier must be held. Secondly, the ball carrier must have any part of his body other than his feet supported by the ground or a player on the ground.

1. A tackled player must immediately pass the ball up to a supporting player or release the ball by placing it on the ground in any direction, or dropping it away from him, or by pushing it away from him — but not in a forward direction.

   After releasing the ball, the tackled player must also get up, or move away from the ball if it is on the ground within a metre of him. Obviously, then, a tackled player may pass from the ground, but it must be immediate — he cannot wait for a supporting player to arrive, he cannot hold onto the ball, nor can he get back on his feet with the ball even if he is no longer held.

2. Likewise the tackler himself must:
   (a) immediately release the tackled player, and
   (b) get up or move away from the tackled player and the ball.

3. A player who is not tackled but goes to the ground out in the open (i.e. the ball is more than 1 m from a player on the ground) to gather a ball or with the ball in his possession, must immediately:
   (a) get up on his feet with the ball, or
   (b) pass the ball, or
   (c) release the ball.
   After he has released the ball he must also get up or move away from the ball.

4. After a tackle all players (including the ball carrier and tackler) must be on their feet before they can play the ball or attempt to tackle another player.

5. No player may:
   (a) prevent a tackled player from passing or releasing the ball or getting up or moving away from the ball. This means the arriving players must allow the ball to be played by the tackled player, providing he plays it immediately.

It often happens that the tackler himself prevents the ball from being played by either hanging on to the ball carrier on the ground or moving his body into such a position as to prevent the ball coming free. The referee will always check what the tackler is doing if the ball fails to come free from a tackle. (See paragraph 2, above.)

(b) pull the ball from a tackled player or pick it up before that player has released it.

(c) while lying on the ground, play or interfere with the ball or opponent in any way. (While on the ground a player is considered out of the play.)

(d) wilfully fall on or over a player or players lying on the ground with the ball near them. Referees will treat all falling over the players on the ground as wilful unless the referee is certain the fall was accidental.

(e) fall on the ball emerging from a scrum or ruck.

(f) go forward of the tackle situation and block or obstruct opponents arriving at the tackle.

6. A try may be scored in a tackle if the tackled player's momentum takes him to the goal line. It may also be scored where the ball carrier can reach out and place the ball on or over the line as part of the tackle 'placing' requirement as described in paragraph 1, above. However, this action must be immediate and in one movement. In this situation a defender is allowed to pull the ball from the tackled player to attempt to stop a try.

A breach of any of the above will result in a penalty.

General

Because of the injury risk in tackles and players on the ground, referees will play little, if any, advantage.

Players not involved in the tackle must try to stay on their feet. Players on the ground must not prevent the ball being freed up and they must get up or move away. In theory there should never be more than two players on the ground during a tackle and release situation.

Dangerous tackles include: charging or knocking a ball carrier over without any attempt to grasp him; early, late, or stiff-arm tackles; tackles around the neck or head; any tackle that in the judgement of the referee is dangerous; or tackling, tapping or pulling the feet of a player jumping for the ball in the open or in a line-out. All dangerous tackles come under the foul play law and as well as a penalty will result in a caution or ordering off.

 The penalty spot for a late tackle is the same as for an early or dangerous tackle, i.e. at the place of infringement. It is only for an obstruction of the kicker, usually by a late charge, that the place is either where the infringement occurred or at the place where the ball landed.

17. SCRUM

PART A: CLUB SENIOR A OR ABOVE

Application

The following laws apply to all international rugby above Under-19 level, Super 12, and all New Zealand men's rugby at or above club Senior A level. Below this level, and for all New Zealand women's rugby, use the New Zealand Domestic Safety Variations in part B of this section.

1. Scrum Formation

 The scrum formation and engagement laws must be strictly complied with to reduce the incidence of serious injury. It is stressed that it is the responsibility of all involved in the game — players, coaches and referees — to ensure that the potential for injury is minimised.

(a) The referee shall mark the place of engagement with his foot before the scrum is formed. The mark can not be closer than 5 m to the touch-line and when close to a goal line, the mark must be such that all feet of the players in the scrum are in the field of play.

(b) A team must not wilfully delay the forming of a scrum. (*Free kick for infringement — FK*)

(c) Eight players shall be required to form a scrum at all times and the number of these players shall not be increased or decreased while the scrum is taking place. All eight players shall remain bound in the scrummage until it ends. (*Penalty kick for infringement — PK*)

Scrum numbers may be reduced only when a team is playing one short for any reason. In this case the opposing scrum has the option of placing the full eight players in the scrum or dropping a player off to match numbers.

Each front row of a scrum shall have three players in it at all times.

(d) Where team numbers are reduced by injuries, ordering offs or unavailability there may never be fewer than five players in either scrum.

(e) 'Golden Oldies': If, during the game, a replacement front row player is required, the referee will set a normal scrum and only if it is clear to him that the front row is no longer safe will he institute 'Golden Oldies' scrums.

Players can avoid having 'Golden Oldies' rules imposed when the opposition is weak by using common sense and not endangering their opponents in the front row by twisting, lowering or popping.

2. Engagement Requirements

(a) Prior to engagement both scrums must be stationary, with the middle line parallel to the goal lines.

(b) Before commencing engagement, each front row must be in a crouched position with heads and shoulders no lower than their hips and so that they are within one arm's length of the opponents' shoulders.

(c) In the interests of safety, each front row must crouch, then pause, and engage only on the call 'Engage' given by the referee. The call 'Engage' is not a command but an indication that the front rows may engage when ready. (*FK*)

(d) Front rows must not engage until the half-back has the ball and is ready to put it in, and the referee has called 'Engage'.

It is dangerous for a front row to form down some distance from its opponents and rush against them. (*PK*)

(e) While the scrum is forming, each front row player's shoulders must not be lower than his hips, and he must adopt a normal stance, with both feet on the ground, and the hooker having his weight firmly on one foot and in a position to hook the ball. (*FK*)

(f) While the scrum is taking place, each front row player must have his weight firmly on at least one foot and be in a position for an effective forward shove, while the shoulders of each person in the scrum must not be lower than his hips. (*FK*)

3. Binding

(a) All front row players must bind firmly and continuously throughout the duration of the scrum. The hooker may bind under or over the props' arms, but he must bind firmly around their bodies at or below the level of the armpits and they must do the same on him.

The hooker must not be so supported that he is not carrying any weight on either foot. (In particular, once the ball is in, he must not try to retrieve the ball from his opponents' scrum with one or both feet by swinging forward on his props.) *(PK)*

(b) The loose-head prop must either bind his opponent with his left arm inside the other prop's right arm, or place his left hand or forearm on his left thigh. He is not permitted to place his hand on the ground. *(PK)*

(c) The tight-head must bind with his right arm outside the left upper arm of his opponent. He must grip that loose-head's jersey — not the sleeve or arm — with his right hand and he must not pull downward. *(PK)*

(d) All players who are not in the front row must throughout the duration of the scrum bind with at least one arm and hand around one of the locks, and each lock must bind on the prop immediately in front of him. Flankers may not hold an opponent with the outer arm. *(FK)*

4. Putting the Ball in

(a) There are a number of laws and circumstances that affect the right of put in for a particular scrum. These are covered in the relevant laws but, as a generalisation, if a scrum has been awarded for things such as knock-ons or forward passes, the non-infringing team shall put the ball in.

Where there has been no infringement — such as breakdowns in play from an indeterminate ruck or tackle — the ball is normally, but not always, put in by the team that was moving forward prior to the stoppage, or, if neither team was moving forward, by the attacking team (the team in the other team's half). The maul law in particular provides clear exceptions to this rule and introduces the concept of the 'turnover' (see section 19).

(b) The ball shall be put in without delay or when ordered by the referee. *(FK)*

Legal binding: loose-head's arm up

Legal binding: loose-head's arm on thigh

Illegal binding: (a) tight-head pulling down,
(b) loose-head's hand on ground

Illegal binding: (a) tight-head gripping sleeve or arm,
(b) loose-head not bound at all

Binding in the scrum: legal and illegal.

(c) The half-back shall:
    (i) stand 1 m from the scrum on the middle line between the two front rows.
    (ii) hold the ball at a level midway between ankle and knee then put it in without delay or feint or backward movement at a quick speed straight along the middle line, so that it first touches the ground immediately beyond the width of the nearest prop's shoulders. (FK)

(d) Play in the scrum begins when the ball leaves the half-back's hands.

(e) If the ball is put in and it comes out at either end of the tunnel without having been touched or played it shall be put in again (although advantage applies as soon as the ball has been put into the scrum and played, i.e. touched). If the ball comes out anywhere else within the scrum play will continue.

(f) If the referee orders the ball to be put in again it must be by the same team.

5. Restrictions on Front Row Players

(a) All front row players must allow a clear tunnel. A player must not prevent the ball being put in or from touching the ground at the required place, nor may he raise or advance a foot until the ball has left the half-back's hands. (FK)

(b) When the ball has touched the ground any front row foot may be used to get the ball, but no front row player may at any time wilfully:
    (i) raise both feet off the ground. (PK)
    (ii) take any position or action by twisting or lowering his body or pulling on an opponent which is likely to cause the scrum to collapse. (PK)
    (iii) kick the ball out of the tunnel in the same direction from which it was put in. (FK)
    (iv) Lift an opponent off his feet or force him upwards out of the scrum ('popping'). (PK)

6. General Restrictions on Players

(a) Players not in the front row may not play the ball while it is in the tunnel, nor may any player return the ball into the scrum — this affects flankers in particular. (FK)

(b) No player may handle the ball in the scrum or pick it up with hands or legs, or wilfully fall or kneel or collapse the scrum, or attempt to gain possession of the ball with any part of the body except the foot or lower leg. (PK)

(c) Neither half-back may take any action whilst the ball is in the scrum to convey to the opponents that the ball is out of the scrum (e.g. dummy pass). (*FK*)

(d) Half-backs may follow the ball around the scrum as long as they do not touch the scrum or get in front of the ball. If they do so advance, opposing flankers may not do anything to prevent them. Neither may the half-back kick the ball while it is in the scrum. (*PK*)

The scrum may be wheeled up to 90°. If this happens the scrum will be set at the same mark and the team that has gained possession shall put in the ball.

7. Scrum Ending

(a) A scrum ends when:
   (i) the ball emerges from the scrum.
   (ii) the number eight detaches and picks up the ball at his feet.
   (iii) the ball in the scrum is on or over the goal line.

   (If this occurs the attacker can now immediately ground the ball and a try may be scored even if the ball is within the confines of the scrum. Likewise a defender can ground the ball and be awarded a touch-down.)

8. IRB Directive

If a scrum collapses the referee must in the interests of safety whistle immediately. It is crucial that the pressure is taken off the collapsed players.

 Whether a scrum offence results in a free kick (*FK*) or a penalty kick (*PK*) appears confusing at first sight. As a general guide, most offences will result in a free kick unless they infringe against laws clearly designed to prevent injury. This is especially true in regard to unsafe binding in the front rows, or wilful collapsing. These (and off-side) will result in a penalty.

OFF-SIDE AT SCRUM

The 'off-side line' means a line parallel to the goal lines through the hindmost foot of the player's team in the scrum.

1. While a scrum is forming or taking place a player is off-side if:
   (a) he joins from his opponents' side, or
   (b) not being in the scrum nor a half-back he:
      (i) fails to retire behind the off-side line, or
      (ii) places either foot in front of the off-side line while the ball is in the scrum.

2. The half-back is off-side if he places his foot in front of the ball while it is in the scrum.

3. (a) Players in the scrum must not leave it until it has ended. This must be noted particularly by flankers and number eights — they must stay bound with the whole length of the arm.
   (b) The number eight is the only player who is permitted to detach but he may only do so if the ball is at his feet. If he does detach he must pick up the ball. On his doing this the scrum has ended. However, it must be noted that he can not simply detach and go into the back line.

4. The non-feeding half-back may stand on the opposite side of the scrum provided he remains behind the hindmost foot (i.e. the off-side line) of his scrum. He may not advance on the opposite side of the scrum to the middle line of the scrum.

In all cases an infringement results in a penalty kick.

PART B: BELOW CLUB SENIOR A

Application

The differences in law outlined apply to all New Zealand club rugby below the Senior A grade and to all women's rugby. All games refereed by volunteer referees and coaches are restricted to 'Golden Oldies' scrums. Only associate referees who have been registered by the NZRFU, and are carrying the NZRFU registration card, are permitted to control scrums under the following laws.

(a) The referee shall mark the place of engagement with his foot before the scrum is formed. The mark cannot be closer than 5 m to the touch-line and no closer than 5 m to a goal line.

(b) Scrum Numbers: Each team must have competent front row players. If they are not able to provide such players prior to the match they shall forfeit the game (see section 2, Player Numbers).

   Eight players (no more, no less) from each team are required to form a scrum at all times.

   When the scrum is in progress players are not permitted to detach and reduce numbers. This particularly affects flankers who must stay fully bound with the whole arm until the scrum ends. If the number eight has the ball at his feet then he may detach but he must pick the ball up.

Where team numbers are reduced by injuries, sin binning, ordering offs or unavailability, there may never be fewer than five players in each scrum and the numbers must always match.

(i) For a full eight-man scrum the 3-4-1 formation must be used with the number eight packing between the locks and the locks packing on each side of the hooker.

(ii) If one player short, a 3-4 formation shall be used.

(iii) If two short, a 3-2-1 formation shall be used.

(iv) If three short, a 3-2 formation shall be used.

If, during the game, a replacement front row player is required, the referee will set a normal scrum and only if it is clear to him that the front row is no longer safe will he institute 'Golden Oldies' scrums.

Players can avoid having 'Golden Oldies' rules imposed when the opposition is weak by using common sense and not endangering their opponents in the front row by twisting, lowering or popping.

Release of the Ball

(a) A scrum must not be wilfully wheeled beyond 45° (FK). If the scrum is otherwise wheeled beyond 45°, the scrum will be reformed at the original place of infringement, the ball to be put in by the side that has gained possession.

(b) The ball must not be held in the scrum for a prolonged period. (FK)

(c) It is not permitted to push the opposing scrum more than 1.5 m from the original mark. (FK)

'Golden Oldies' Scrums

'Golden Oldies' scrums must have eight players per side in them and are not contested, the team putting the ball in must hook it, and neither team is permitted to push. All players must stay bound to the scrum until the ball emerges.

OFF-SIDE AT SCRUM

Half-backs are not permitted to cross the middle line of the scrum. (PK)

18. RUCK

A ruck can take place only in the field-of-play, not in in-goal. It is formed when the ball is on the ground and one or more players from each team are on their feet, and in physical contact, closing around the ball between them. Therefore, only two (opposing) players are required as the minimum for a ruck.

Rucking is now defined in law. In essence it requires a player to ruck only for the ball itself. For him to be rucking legally, the ball must be in the immediate vicinity of the player's feet. He may not jump on or trample players on the ground. He must attempt to step over and not on them. He has an onus of safety for the player on the ground. It must be emphasised that for legitimate rucking to occur the ball must be on the ground. If the ball is not on the ground then there is no ruck and the hands — not the feet — must be used to free it up.

1. A ruck ends when:
   (a) the ball emerges.
   (b) the ball is on or over the goal line.

2. A player forming, joining or participating in a ruck must have his head and shoulders no lower than his hips and must bind with at least one full arm length (from hand to shoulder) around the body of a player of his team in the ruck. (*Free kick for infringement — FK*)

   Players must join a ruck from the back and not the side. (*Penalty kick for infringement — PK*)

3. A player must not:
   (a) return the ball into the ruck. (*FK*)
   (b) handle the ball in the ruck except in the act of grounding for a try or touch-down (see 1. (b), above). (*PK*)
   (c) pick up the ball in the ruck by hand or legs. (*PK*)
   (d) wilfully collapse the ruck. (*PK*)
   (e) jump on other players in the ruck. (*PK*)
   (f) wilfully fall or kneel in the ruck. (*PK*)

(g) while lying on the ground interfere in any way with the ball in, or emerging from, the ruck; he must do his best to roll away from it. (*PK*)

(h) ruck an opponent or pull him out of the ruck, even if he is off-side. (*PK*)

Neither half-back may take any action whilst the ball is in the ruck to convey to the opponents that the ball is out of the ruck (e.g dummy pass). (*FK*)

Indeterminate Rucks

Should the ball in a ruck become unplayable then the put in to the resulting scrum will go to the team that was moving forward immediately prior to the stoppage.

'Moving forward' does not mean 'collapsing forward'. If a team has been driving forward and the ball subsequently becomes unplayable then they will still get the put in regardless of which way the ruck finally collapsed.

If neither team was moving forward immediately prior to the stoppage then the team that was moving forward immediately prior to the formation of the ruck will get the put in. This situation occurs mostly at the tackle situation which is the primary cause of rucks.

If neither of these situations applies then the referee will award the scrum to the attacking team. ('Attacking' is defined as being in the opponents' half.)

OFF-SIDE AT RUCK OR MAUL

The 'off-side line' means a line parallel to the goal lines through the hindmost foot of the player's team in the ruck or maul.

1. Ruck or Maul other than at Line-Out

While a ruck or maul is taking place (including a ruck or maul which continues after a line-out has ended) a player is off-side if he:

(a) joins it from his opponents' side, or

(b) joins it in front of his hindmost team-mate in the ruck or maul.

(c) does not join the ruck or maul but fails to retire behind the off-side line without delay, or

(d) unbinds from the ruck or leaves the maul and does not immediately either rejoin it on or alongside the hindmost player, or retire behind the off-side line, or

(e) advances beyond the off-side line with either foot and does not join the ruck or maul.

All result in a penalty kick at the place of infringement.

2. Ruck or Maul at Line-Out

A player 'participating in the line-out' (that is, any player in the two lines, the thrower and his immediate opponent, and the two half-backs) is not obliged to join or remain in the ruck or maul and if he is not in the ruck or maul he continues to participate in the line-out until the line-out has ended.

While a line-out is in progress and a ruck or maul takes place, a player is off-side if he:

(a) joins the ruck or maul from his opponents' side, or

(b) joins it in front of his hindmost team-mate in the ruck or maul, or

(c) being a player who is participating in the line-out and is not in the ruck or maul, does not retire to and remain at the off-side line (hindmost foot), or

(d) being a player who is not participating in the line-out, remains or advances within 10 m of the line-of-touch, or forward of the player's goal line if that is closer.

Infringement of (a), (b) or (c) results in a penalty 15 m from touch along the line-of-touch, while for (d) the penalty is on the offending team's 10 metre off-side line opposite the place of infringement but not less than 15 m from the touch-line and not less than 5 m from the offender's goal line. If several offenders are off-side the kick is given in the place most favourable to the other team. The provisions of (d), above, also apply to non-participating players generally (see Off-side at Line-Out, paragraph 2, page 62).

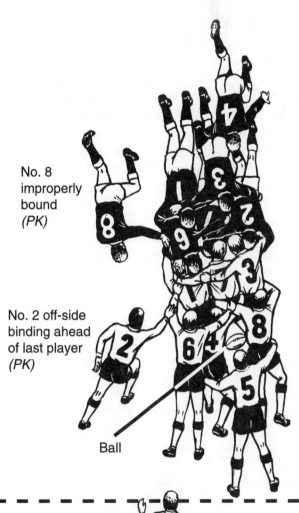

No. 8
improperly
bound
(PK)

No. 2 off-side
binding ahead
of last player
(PK)

Ball

No. 9 on-side

No.11 off-side:
ahead of last foot
if not joining
ruck/maul *(PK)*

Some ruck and maul infringements.

19. MAUL

Understanding how and when a maul is formed and when it ends is very important for coaches and players wanting to use the opportunities this law provides for continuity of play at second phase.

A maul can take place only in the field-of-play and not in in-goal. It is formed by one or more players from each team, on their feet and in physical contact, closing around a player who is carrying the ball. Therefore, a minimum of three players are needed to form a maul (i.e. the ball carrier, the opponent and another player from the ball carrier's team).

1. A maul ends when:
   (a) the ball in the maul is on or over the goal line.
   (b) the ball or ball carrier emerges from the maul.
   (c) the ball is on the ground (i.e. it becomes a defined ruck with the bulk of the players still on their feet).
   (d) the referee blows his whistle.

 Should a maul collapse downwards with the bulk of players off their feet and the ball on the ground, it is still a maul, albeit a collapsed one, and not a ruck. The turnover law still applies.

2. A player joining a maul must have his head and shoulders no lower than his hips. He must enter the maul from the back and not join it from the side.

3. A player is not in physical contact unless he is caught in or bound to the maul and not merely alongside it. This is especially important, and as with rucks and scrums he must be bound with the full length of at least one arm or risk being off-side. Holding another player with just a hand is not enough.

4. A player must not:
   (a) jump on players in a maul. (*Penalty kick for infringement — PK*)

(b) wilfully collapse a maul or attempt to take the legs out from under any player in the maul. *(PK)*

(c) attempt to drag an opponent out of a maul, even if that player is on his opponents' side of it. *(PK)*

Neither half-back may take any action whilst the ball is in the maul to convey to the opponents that the ball is out of the maul (e.g. dummy pass). *(Free kick for infringement — FK)*

5. The referee will allow a brief time for the ball to emerge if the maul becomes stationary or the ball appears trapped.

    If, however, the ball becomes unplayable, or it appears it will probably not emerge without delay, the referee should not allow prolonged wrestling for the ball but should order a scrum.

    The put in will go to the side not in possession at the commencement of the maul (i.e. a turnover occurs).

    The referee will be checking which team had possession at the moment the ball carrier was bound by a team-mate and an opponent (the minimum requirement for the formation of a maul). What happens to the ball after that is of no relevance for deciding who gets the put in.

    The onus is on the ball carrier and his team to do something constructive or risk losing the put in at any ensuing scrum.

    If the referee cannot decide which team had possession at the commencement of the maul, then the scrum feed will go to the team moving forward prior to the whistle. If there was no movement then it will go to the attacking team ('attacking' is defined as territorial, i.e. the team that is in the other team's half).

6. There is one exception to the preceding paragraph 5. This involves a player catching the ball directly from an opponent's kick, other than at a kick-off or drop-out. In these circumstances, if a player catches the ball and is then immediately held so that a maul occurs, then if that maul does not subsequently end or the ball emerge, or the maul becomes stationary, then the receiving team will get the put in for the subsequent scrum.

OFF-SIDE AT MAUL

The laws for off-side at the maul are identical to those of the ruck off-side (see section 18, Ruck).

20. TOUCH AND LINE-OUT

Laws 23 and 24D

Touch

The ball is in touch when:

(a) it is not being carried and it comes into contact with a touch-line or the ground, or a person or object on or beyond it. (If the ball in the air crosses the touch-line but is blown or curves back and lands in the playing area, without touching anything on the way, it is not in touch.)

(There are some other subtleties when the ball is, or is not, in touch and who gets the subsequent throw-in. These are beyond the scope of this publication.)

(b) being carried, it or the player carrying it touches the touch-line or the ground beyond.

Line-Out

The mark for a line-out may be no closer than 1 m to a goal line.

The line-of-touch is an imaginary line in the field-of-play at right angles to the touch-line through the place where the ball is to be thrown in and stretches from one side of the field to the other.

A scrum ordered during a line-out is awarded 15 m in, along the line-of-touch, as are any line-out free kicks or penalty kicks against players participating in the line-out.

 Free kicks awarded at the line-out are generally for technical offences, particularly in the formation stage, such as numbers, spacing and where players in the line-out stand. Penalty kicks are for play such as pushing, charging, holding, obstructing, and off-side.

1. Formation of the Line-Out

(a) A line-out is formed by at least two players from each team standing in a single line on each side of the line-of-touch. The team throwing in decides the maximum number. Such players are those 'in the line-out'. The opposition may line up fewer players but not more. (*Free kick for infringement — FK*)

   If the throwing team lines up less than the normal number of players, their opponents must be given a reasonable chance to conform. Retiring players must do so without delay to a line 10 m behind the line-of-touch. Only when the line-out ends (see paragraph 4 below) may they rejoin play. (*FK*)

(b) Each team must line up so as to leave a clear space of 1 m between the two lines of players, at the shoulders. This space should be maintained (unless in a genuine act of jumping for the ball) until the ball has touched a player or the ground. Even allowing for the jump the jumper may not step across the line-of-touch in the attempt. There is no set distance between team-mates. (*FK*)

(c) The line-out extends from 5 m from touch to 15 m in. Any player at this stage who is lined up but further than 15 m back when the line-out begins is not in the line-out. (*FK*)

2. Place of the Line-Out

(a) (i) When the ball goes either directly or indirectly into touch from any kick, including a penalty kick, or free kick within 22 m of the kicker's goal line, the line-out occurs where the ball went into touch.
   (ii) However, if the ball goes out on the full from any kick, other than a penalty kick, taken outside of the kicker's 22 metre area or from a kick by a player who has retreated behind his 22 metre line before taking the kick, the line-out occurs opposite where the ball was kicked. If the ball goes directly into touch after travelling backwards from the kick then the line-out is where it went into touch (normal advantage applies).
   (iii) On all other occasions the line-out is where the ball or ball carrier went into touch.

(b) When the ball is kicked into touch from a penalty kick, the ball will be thrown in by the team which took the penalty kick.

(c) In the event of doubt as to which team should throw in, the attacking team shall do so.

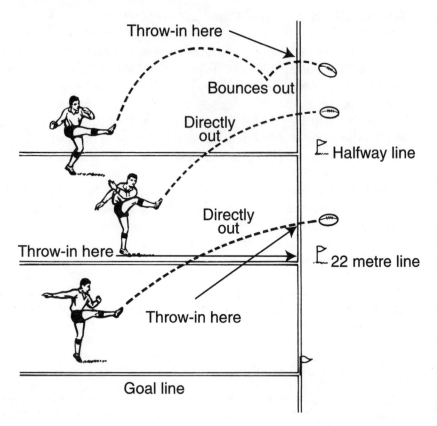

Place of the line-out.

(d) The ball must be thrown in without delay or feint. (*FK*)

(e) If the ball is wilfully or repeatedly not thrown in straight a penalty kick will be awarded.

(f) Whether at a formed line-out or a quick throw-in, the ball must be thrown in correctly, i.e. straight, at least 5 m, and with the thrower's feet entirely in touch. If the ball has not been thrown in correctly, the opposing team may opt for another line-out or a scrum, their ball.

3. Quick Throw-In

A quick throw-in without waiting for players to line up is permitted under special conditions.

It is important to understand the difference between a quick throw-in and a quick line-out. Once two players from each team have lined up then a line-out is formed and the normal line-out rules apply, even if the throw-in occurs quickly. However, if the line-out is not 'formed', i.e. there are less than two players from each side lined up, then a quick throw-in is permitted and many of the restrictions of a normal line-out, such as off-side lines, do not apply.

A quick throw-in may be taken from any point along the touch-line between where the ball went into touch and the goal line of the team throwing in the ball, provided:

(i) the ball that went into touch is used, and

(ii) it has been touched by no one other than the player throwing it in. (The ball striking a spectator or player is OK so long as it is not intentionally touched.)

(iii) the ball must still be thrown in straight and must travel 5 m before being played.

At a quick throw-in, if the ball is not thrown in correctly then, at the opponents' option, the resulting scrum or line-out will occur where the quick throw-in was attempted. This of course may be further downfield than where the ball actually went into touch. This provides an incentive for the team taking the quick throw-in to do it correctly.

4. Beginning and End of Line-Out

(a) No player may jump for the ball or support any player before the ball has left the hands of the player throwing it in. The line-out begins when the ball leaves the thrower's hands.

(b) The line-out ends when:

(i) a ruck or maul develops and all feet of the players in the ruck or maul have moved beyond the line-of-touch, or

(ii) a player carrying the ball leaves the line-out, or

(iii) the ball has been passed, knocked back or kicked from the line-out, or

(iv) the ball is thrown beyond a position 15 m from the touch-line, or

(v) the ball becomes unplayable and play is stopped.

It is important for backs and any forwards not participating in a formed line-out to realise that unless and until a line-out ends in one of these ways, they must not approach within 10 m of the line-of-touch. (*Penalty kick for infringement — PK, 10 m back from line-of-touch.*)

5. Peeling Off

(a) This is when a player moves from his position in the line-out to catch the ball when it has been passed or knocked back by a team-mate in the line-out (also known in New Zealand as the 'Willie Away'). He must move parallel and close to the line-out and may stop to receive the ball.

(b) When the ball is in touch, players forming a line-out may not leave the line-out when formed until the line-out has ended (*FK*), except:

(i) in a peeling off movement (but the player must not begin to peel off until the ball has left the thrower's hands), or

(ii) at a quick throw-in, when a player may approach or leave the line-of-touch without penalty, or

(iii) the non-throwing team reduces their numbers (see paragraph 1, above).

Players may, however, change their position in the line-out prior to the ball being thrown in.

6. Restrictions on Players in Line-Out

When a line-out is taking place (i.e. the ball has left the hands of the player throwing it in) any player in the line-out must not:

(i) be off-side. (*PK*)

(ii) hold, push, charge, shoulder, or obstruct an opponent not holding the ball. (*PK*)

(iii) use an opponent as support to enable him to jump for the ball. (*PK*)

(iv) charge an opponent except in an attempt to tackle him or play the ball. (*PK*)

(v) lift a player of his own team off the ground. (*FK*)

(vi) support a player of his own team before the player has jumped for the ball. (*FK*)

(vii) stand within 5 m of the touch-line or prevent the ball from being thrown 5 m. (*FK*)

When jumping for the ball a player must use both hands or his inside arm to catch or deflect the ball. A player who has both hands above his head is permitted to use either hand to play the ball. (*FK*)

A player may move in-field beyond the 15 metre mark only to gather a long throw and only after it has left the thrower's hands. (*PK*)

The 1 m gap between opponents applies until the ball has touched the ground or a player, but players in the act of jumping for the ball are exempt provided they do not step across the line-of-touch. (*PK*)

The difference between (v) 'lifting' and (vi) 'supporting' is a subtle one and difficult to referee. A jumper must get off the ground unaided. Once that occurs he may be supported.

7. Restrictions on Players Not in Line-Out

Such players, of either team, may not advance until the line-out ends in the defined way (see paragraph 4 above).

They may only move from behind the off-side line and take the ball from the throw-in in the following ways:

(a) a player lawfully advancing at a long throw-in (see the following description, Off-Side at Line-Out). (*PK*)

(b) a player 'participating in the line-out' (as defined in Off-Side at Line-Out) may run into a gap in the (usually shortened) line-out and take the ball provided he does not charge or obstruct any player in the line-out and he has rejoined the line-out before the ball is thrown. (*PK*)

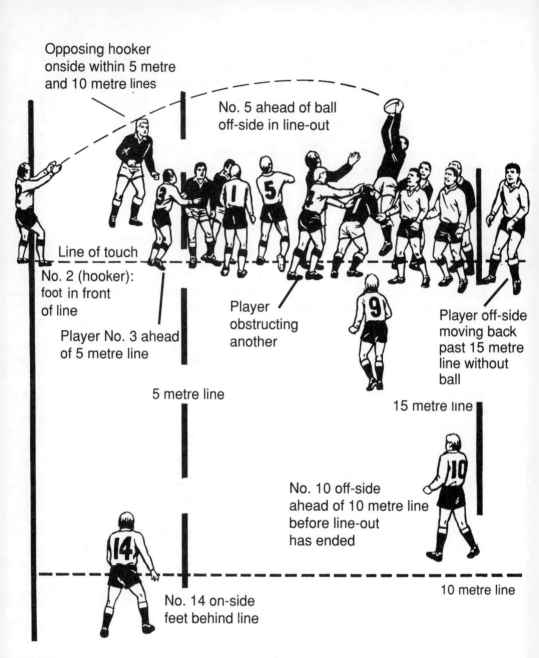

Opposing hooker onside within 5 metre and 10 metre lines

No. 5 ahead of ball off-side in line-out

Line of touch

No. 2 (hooker): foot in front of line

Player No. 3 ahead of 5 metre line

Player obstructing another

Player off-side moving back past 15 metre line without ball

5 metre line

15 metre line

No. 10 off-side ahead of 10 metre line before line-out has ended

No. 14 on-side feet behind line

10 metre line

Some typical line-out infringements.

OFF-SIDE AT LINE-OUT

There are four different off-side lines associated with the line-out, depending on whether players are participating in the line-out or not, and depending on the stage the line-out is at.

(a) The line-of-touch.

(b) A line determined by the ball.

(c) The line through the hindmost foot of any ruck or maul taking place during a line-out.

(d) The line 10 m behind the line-of-touch and parallel to the goal lines, or the goal line itself if that is nearer.

In addition, players may be penalised for being within 5 m of touch or beyond 15 m from touch (see paragraph 1. (a) (iii) below).

The players 'participating in the line-out' are those in the two lines, the ball thrower and his immediate opponent, and the two half-backs.

1. Off-Side while Participating in Line-Out

(a) A participating player is off-side if:

(i) before the ball has touched a player or the ground, he is in front of the line-of-touch with either foot.

(ii) after the ball has touched a player or the ground, if he is not carrying the ball, he advances with either foot in front of the ball unless he is legally attempting to tackle an opponent, but such tackle must start from his side of the ball.

(iii) before the line-out ends, he moves beyond 15 m from the touch-line. However, players of the throwing team may move beyond the 15 m mark for a long throw-in to them, but only when the ball leaves the thrower's hands, and if they do, their opponents in the line-out may follow them. If players do move infield and the ball is not thrown to or beyond them, they are penalised for off-side.

(b) After the throw, the thrower and his immediate opponent must either remain within 5 m of the touch-line, retire to the 10 metre off-side line or join the line-out. If the thrower is not the wing, the wing must retire to the off-side line 10 m back.

2. Off-Side While Not Participating in Line-Out

(a) A non-participating player is off-side if he moves within 10 m of the line-of-touch before the line-out is ended.

(b) However, non-participating players of the thrower's team may advance for a long throw-in to them beyond the line-out but only after the ball leaves the thrower's hands, and if they do, their opponents may advance also.

(c) If players advance but the ball is not thrown to them they will be penalised on the 10 metre off-side line at the place of infringement, but at least 15 m in from touch.

Players arriving at their positions after the ball has been thrown in will not be penalised so long as they return on-side without interfering and without delay.

21. OFF-SIDE AND ON-SIDE IN GENERAL PLAY

Laws 24A and 25

 Because general play is undefined in law, it is important to be able to recognise what it is. General play is taken to mean any play that is not covered by a specific legal definition such as a ruck, maul, line-out, or scrum.

Off-side means that a player is in a position in which he is out of the game and is liable to penalty. To be actually penalised, an off-side player normally has to take some further action.

In general play, a player is off-side because he is in front of the ball when it has been last played by another member of his own team.

At the set pieces such as the scrum, ruck, maul or line-out, a player is usually off-side because he remains or advances in front of the lines or places specifically defined for each of those situations (see the relevant sections).

1. A player is in an off-side position in general play if the ball has been kicked or touched or is being carried by one of his team behind him.

2. There is no penalty for merely being in an off-side position. An off-side player will be penalised only:
   (a) if he plays the ball or obstructs an opponent.
   (b) if from a kick he remains within 10 m of an opponent waiting to play the ball or the place where the ball lands (see the following paragraph 7).
   (c) if he is outside the 10 metre circle and advances towards an opponent waiting to play the ball before he is put on-side, either by his own team, or the opponent himself (see illustration, page 66). In this situation he must either retire or stand still. He cannot move upfield (this is commonly referred to as the 'downtown' rule).

Exceptions:
(i) An off-side player is accidentally off-side when he can not avoid being touched by the ball or ball carrier. Play continues unless the infringing team gains an advantage, in which case a scrum is set. If the player was considered wilfully off-side, then a penalty will be awarded. A player taking the ball from a team-mate behind him should likewise be penalised.
(ii) A player who receives an unintentional forward pass is not off-side (but the receiver of a team-mate's knock-on is penalised if it deprives the other team of an advantage).

3. A player can be off-side in his in-goal.

4. Referees will usually play advantage with off-side if the non-offending team gains or appears likely to gain advantage, but not when an opponent waiting to receive the ball is likely to be 'taken out' by an off-side player charging within the 10 metre circle.

It is essential that players understand that if they become off-side in general play, they can be put on-side in various ways by actions of either team-mates or opponents. The exception to this is the player within the 10 metre circle (see paragraph 7).

6. If the ball is kicked into touch, an off-side player may advance but only when the referee or touch judge has signalled that the ball is out. If the off-side player advances before this he will be penalised, especially if he restricts the opponents' opportunity for a quick throw-in to the subsequent line-out.

7. **The 10 Metre Circle**
Whenever a team kicks the ball downfield and there is an opponent waiting to catch it then that opponent has an imaginary circle of 10 m in diameter thrown around him by the referee. This circle is a safety zone that is there to protect that player from being knocked down by an off-side player following up illegally.

It also applies to the place where the ball lands or pitches. Again, the imaginary 10 metre circle is applied by the referee around that spot.

The law actually states that there is no penalty for being in an off-side position unless:

'he being within ten metres of an opponent waiting to play the ball or of the place where the ball pitches does not retire without delay and without interfering with the opponent ... '

So regardless of where a player is within the 10 metre circle he must make the quickest exit possible from it without interfering with an opponent — and that may be towards the opponent's goal line if he is behind the opponent. He simply cannot stand there. He must attempt to retire by the shortest possible route.

The other crucial part is that a player within a 10 metre circle can never be put on-side by anyone other than himself unless he is actively retiring out of the 10 metre circle. Standing within the 10 metre circle with raised hands is no protection from a penalty. The player must actually retire. This is especially relevant when a half-back puts in a short kick over the heads of his forwards at set plays like line-outs or scrums.

On all other occasions in the game a player can be put on-side by actions of his team-mates or even his opponents.

There is an important subtlety here, though, and this is in the case where a kick is charged down and members of the kicker's team are closer than 10 m to the opponent who did the charge down. On the face of it, it would appear that these players cannot be put on-side and must retire 10 m away from the ball. However, the law has ruled that because the charger was not 'waiting to play the ball' then he is not entitled to a 10 metre circle protection so the kicker's team can re-enter the game immediately.

The other important aspect about this is the fact that the 10 metre circle is so large. Referees themselves have to learn how to picture the circle clearly and understand just how big it is and that a player really has to make some positive actions to get out of it. The illustration on page 67 will clearly illustrate its size, and players can forfeit a large amount of territory if they do not appreciate its significance.

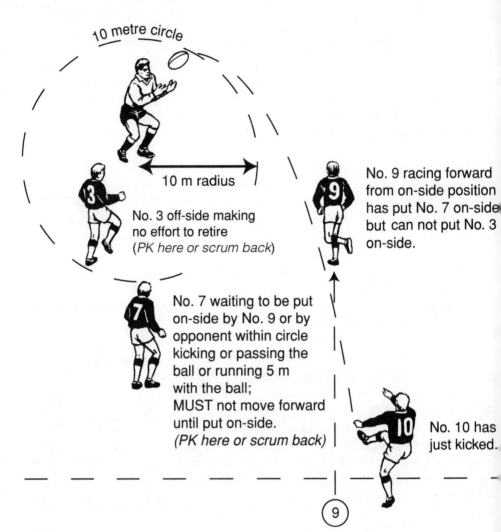

10 metre circle

10 m radius

No. 3 off-side making
no effort to retire
(PK here or scrum back)

No. 9 racing forward
from on-side position
has put No. 7 on-side
but can not put No. 3
on-side.

No. 7 waiting to be put
on-side by No. 9 or by
opponent within circle
kicking or passing the
ball or running 5 m
with the ball;
MUST not move forward
until put on-side.
(PK here or scrum back)

No. 10 has
just kicked.

9

Some typical on-side and off-side situations in general play.

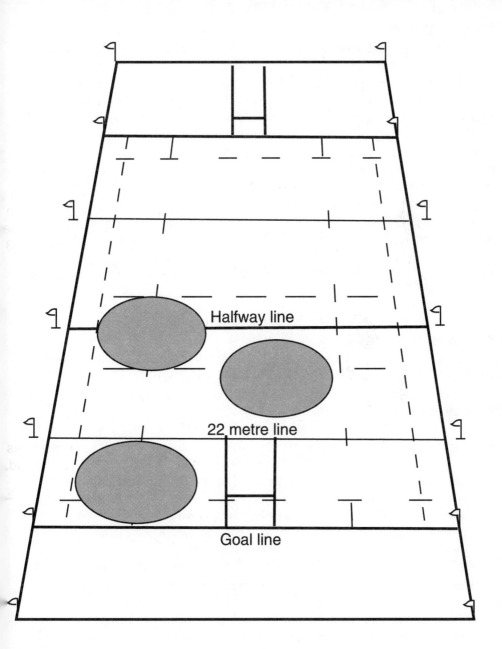

Halfway line

22 metre line

Goal line

Examples of the 10 metre circle to scale (note the large area it covers).

Place of Penalty

This can be a little confusing. If a player is off-side in general play, the penalty kick is subject to some options.

For the player in the 10 metre circle, the non-offending team has the option of taking a penalty kick at the place where the offside player failed to retire out of the 10 metre circle or of taking a scrum back from where the ball was kicked.

However, in the case where a player advances downfield to follow up a kick before he has been put on-side, the place for the penalty kick is again an option for the non-offending team. In this circumstance the option is a penalty kick at the place from where the player first advanced illegally or a scrum back at the place from where the ball was kicked.

This is an important distinction and could be a much heavier penalty in terms of field position than a 10 metre circle breach. The offending player could be much closer to the kicker than the opponent waiting downfield to receive the kick. The subsequent penalty could prove very costly if it occurs when the offending player is anywhere in his own half.

ON-SIDE (Law 25)

This is a law that is little understood, but it is very important because it opens up a whole range of tactical options if played correctly.

Off-side players can get back on-side in three different ways:
• by actions of their own.
• by actions of their own team-mates.
• by actions of their opponents.

On-side simply means a player is in the game and can fully participate in it.

1. Player Made On-Side by Actions of his Own Team

(a) Any player who is off-side in general play becomes on-side as a result of any of the following actions of his own team when:

(i) the off-side player has retired behind the player of his team who last kicked, touched or carried the ball (behind the player, not the place), or

(ii) one of his team carrying the ball has run in front of him, or

(iii) one of his team (it need not be the kicker) has run in front of him after coming from the place or behind the place where the ball was kicked (see paragraph 7 above for the exception to this when within the 10 metre circle).

2. Player Made On-Side by Actions of Opposing Team

(a) Any player who is off-side in general play and further away than 10 m from his opponent waiting to catch the ball becomes on-side when:

(i)   an opponent carrying the ball has run 5 m, or

(ii) an opponent kicks or passes the ball, or

(iii) an opponent intentionally touches the ball and does not catch or gather it (e.g. drops a catch or charges the ball down).

(b) An off-side player in the 10 metre circle can not be put on-side by any action of his opponents.

Any other player in general play is always put on-side when an opponent plays the ball as in 2 (a) above.

3. Players Retiring at Scrum, Ruck, Maul or Line-Out

(a) A player who is off-side when a scrum, ruck, maul or line-out is forming or taking place and is retiring as required becomes on-side when:

(i) an opponent carrying the ball has run 5 m, or

(ii) an opponent has kicked the ball.

An off-side player in this situation is not put on-side when an opponent passes the ball.

(b) Wilful loiterers must not prevent or hinder opponents from playing the ball in any way. When a team has gained quick possession from a scrum, ruck, maul or line-out and starts a passing movement, opponents who are retiring must not interfere with the movement unless an opponent has kicked or run 5 m with the ball.

22. FOUL PLAY

Foul play is any action by a player which is contrary to the letter and spirit of the game and includes obstruction, unfair play, misconduct, dangerous play, unsporting behaviour, retaliation, and repeated and wilful infringements.

Foul play offences result in a penalty kick and can also result in a caution, temporary suspension ('sin bin') or ordering off, and a penalty try if appropriate.

In general, a penalty is awarded at the place of infringement, except:

(a) for offences in in-goal (where not covered by (c) or (d) below; see section 10, In-Goal, 2 (c)).

(b) for offences in touch, the penalty is awarded 15 m in from touch.

(c) for offences while the ball is out of play, including in-goal, the penalty is taken wherever play would otherwise restart.

(d) for a wilful obstruction or the late charge of a player who has just kicked the ball, the option is given of a kick at the place of infringement or where the ball lands.

This provision is subject to the kick being awarded no closer than 15 m from touch or 5 m from the goal line should the ball go into touch or in-goal

1. Obstruction

It is illegal for any player:

(a) who is running for the ball to charge or push an opponent also running for the ball, except shoulder to shoulder.

(b) who is in an off-side position wilfully to run or stand in front of another player of his team who is carrying the ball, thus preventing an opponent reaching the ball carrier.

(c) who is carrying the ball after it has come out of a scrum, ruck, maul or line-out to attempt to force or drive his way through the players of his team in front of him.

(d) to obstruct a half-back coming round the scrum (this applies in particular to flankers and the number eight).

There are no circumstances in which a ball carrier himself can be penalised for obstruction.

2. Unfair Play, Repeated Infringements
It is illegal for any player:

(a) deliberately to play unfairly or wilfully infringe any law of the game. There is growing concern among referees that the game is being subjected to the 'professional' foul where the laws are deliberately broken to prevent an opponent from scoring. This is a serious offence and will always incur at least a penalty kick, but more often than not will result in the sin binning of the offender. (*Penalty kick for infringement — PK*)

(b) wilfully to waste time. (*Free kick for infringement — FK*)

(c) wilfully to knock or throw the ball from the playing area into touch, touch-in-goal, or over the dead-ball line. (*PK*)

(d) to infringe repeatedly any law of the game. (*PK*)

The higher the grade the stricter the referee will be, and may caution or send off a repeated offender.

3. Misconduct, Dangerous Play
It is illegal for any player:

(a) to strike an opponent, even in retaliation. (*PK*)

(b) wilfully or recklessly to hack or kick an opponent or to trip him with a foot or to trample an opponent lying on the ground. (*PK*)

(c) to tackle early, late or dangerously, including a stiff-arm tackle (see section 16, Tackle). (*PK*)

The following actions are deemed to be dangerous play:
  • If a player charges or knocks down an opponent carrying the ball without any attempt to grasp him.
  • If a player taps or pulls the foot or feet of another player who is jumping in a line-out.
  • If a player attempts to tackle a player who, when fielding a kick in open play, is off the ground jumping for the ball.

(d) who is not running for the ball wilfully or recklessly to charge or obstruct an opponent who has just kicked the ball. (*PK*)

(e) to hold, push, charge, obstruct or grasp an opponent not holding the ball except in a scrum, ruck or maul. ('Off the ball' play is included here and often occurs at a tackle or other breakdown before a ruck or maul has formed.) (*PK*)

Except in a scrum or ruck the dragging away of a player lying close to the ball is permitted. Otherwise pulling any part of the clothing of an opponent is 'holding'.

(f) in the front row of a scrum to form down some distance from the opponents and rush against them. (*PK*)

(g) wilfully or recklessly to cause a scrum, ruck or maul to collapse or to force an opponent up out of the scrum ('popping'). (*PK*)

(h) while the ball is out of play to molest, obstruct or in any way interfere with an opponent or be guilty of any form of misconduct. (*PK*)

Typical situations here would include throwing the ball away to prevent a quick throw-in or penalty kick, interfering with a player trying to take a quick drop-out, or abuse of the referee.

(i) to commit any misconduct on the playing area which is prejudicial to the spirit of good sportsmanship. This very broadly worded clause would include bad language. (*PK*)

Referees are instructed to be severe on foul play, especially misconduct or dangerous play, and an offender should be ordered off, sin binned or else cautioned he will be sent off if he repeats the offence. Once a caution has been issued a player who offends again under any of the foul play provisions must be sent off.

4. Temporary Suspension ('Sin Bin')

(a) Within New Zealand rugby at all levels, a player guilty of foul play, misconduct or repeated infringements shall either be ordered off, sent off the field-of-play for up to five minutes (sin binned) or else cautioned that he will be sent off if he repeats the offence. In Super 12, sin binning is for up to ten minutes.

For a similar offence, after a caution or temporary suspension, the player must be ordered off.

(b) If sin binned, a player must remain behind his opponent's dead-ball line and must not enter the in-goal area or field-of-play until permitted by the referee to resume playing.

(c) The sin bin is not a substitute for ordering off. If the offence warrants it, the player must be ordered off.

(d) Time is to be counted from when the player reaches his opponents' dead-ball line. Weather conditions should be taken into account in determining the time.

(e) If the period in the sin-bin has not expired when half-time or full time is called, the period is then considered to have expired.

(f) In all New Zealand domestic rugby, from Ranfurly Shield down, when a front row player is either sin binned or ordered off the field he may be replaced. If this should occur then another member of that team must leave the field of play (see section 2, Player Numbers).

(g) If, during the game, a replacement front row player is required through injury, sin binning, or ordering off, the referee will set a normal scrum. Only if it is clear to him that the front row is no longer safe will he institute 'Golden Oldies' scrummaging.

 Players can avoid having 'Golden Oldies' rules imposed when the opposition is weak by using common sense and not endangering their opponents in the front row.

5. Player Ordered Off

A player who is ordered off shall take no further part in the match. The referee will send a report to the union naming the player and describing the circumstances. The union will investigate the matter and take such action and inflict such penalty as they see fit.

6. Player 'Cited'

Any player who has been cited may not play again until his case has been heard or he has been given specific dispensation to play by the judicial committee responsible for hearing his case.

23. SEVEN-A-SIDE RUGBY

The growth in popularity of seven-a-side rugby over the last few years has been spectacular and it has proved an excellent training vehicle for the skills and attacking flair of quality players.

In recognition of this, the International Rugby Board has introduced formal rules for the game of sevens and they are now an internationally recognised part of the game.

The following laws are those affecting the sevens game and should be read in conjunction with the main laws of the game.

Law 3: Number of Players
- Team numbers are restricted to seven with a maximum of three replacements/ substitutions.
- Players who have been substituted can not replace an injured player except in the case of the 'blood bin'.

Law 4: Toss and Time
- The duration of play in all matches other than in a competition final shall not exceed 14 minutes.
- Play shall be divided into two halves of seven minutes. At the interval, which should not exceed one minute, the teams shall change ends.
- The duration of play in a competition final shall not exceed 20 minutes. Play shall be divided into two halves of ten minutes. At the interval, which should not exceed two minutes, the teams shall change ends.
- Where there is a drawn match and extra time is required, the extra time shall be played in periods of five minutes. After each period the team shall change ends without interval.
- Before commencement of extra time the captains shall toss for the right to kick off or the choice of ends.
- In extra time the team which scores first will immediately be declared the winner without further play.
- A period not exceeding one minute shall be allowed for treatment of an injury to a player or for any other permitted delay. A longer period may be allowed only if the additional time is required for the removal of an injured player from the playing area.

Law 6: Referee and Touch Judges

There are two in-goal judges for every match. One will officiate at each end of the ground in the in-goal area. Their control by the referee and their responsibilities are the same as for touch judges except that their area of responsibility is limited to the in-goal.

Law 10: Kick-Off

- After a team has scored they will take the kick-off. The ball must be kicked from the correct place and by the correct form of kick, otherwise it shall be kicked off again.
- The ball must reach the opponents' 10 metre line, unless played first by an opponent. If the ball reaches the 10 metre line and is then blown back, play shall continue.
  Penalty: Free kick at the centre of the halfway line.

- The ball must not be kicked directly into touch.
  Penalty: Free kick at the centre of the halfway line.

Law 13: Kick at Goal after a Try

- If the scoring team elects to take a kick at goal after a try it shall be a drop kick on a line through the place where the try was scored.
- The opposing team must assemble immediately within reasonable proximity of its own 10 metre line.

Law 20: Scrum

Three players from each team shall be required to form a front row which is a scrummage and shall remain bound until it ends. The head of a player in the front row shall not be next to the head of a player of the same team. (*Penalty kick for infringement — PK*)

Law 27: Penalty Kick

A penalty kick is a kick awarded to the non-offending team as stated in the laws.

It may be taken by any player of the non-offending team and by any form of kick, except a place kick. The kicker, if holding the ball, must propel it out of his hands or, if the ball is on the ground, he must propel it a visible distance from the mark.

24. TOURNAMENT RULES

The following special rules apply to the U-BIX Rugby Super 12, Air New Zealand National Provincial Championships (NPC), Philips Tri-Nations, 5 Nations and Rugby World Cup competitions.

TEMPORARY SUSPENSION (SIN BIN)

Tournament	In Force	Duration	Location
NPC	Yes	10 minutes	Halfway line
Super 12	Yes	10 minutes	Halfway line
Tri-Nations	Yes	10 minutes	Halfway line
5 Nations	No	—	—

RED AND YELLOW CARDS

Tournament	In Force
NPC	Yes
Super 12	Yes
Tri-Nations	Yes
5 Nations	Yes

 At the time of writing, the Rugby World Cup Committee had yet to finalise policy regarding temporary suspension and the use of red and yellow cards for the 1999 Rugby World Cup.

MATCH POINTS

Tournament	Win	Draw	Loss	4-Try Bonus
NPC	4	2	(within 7) 1	1
Super 12	4	2	(within 7) 1	1
Tri-Nations	4	2	(within 7) 1	1
5 Nations	3	2	nil	nil
Rugby World Cup	3	2	1	nil

DETERMINING TOURNAMENT OUTCOMES

When a decision needs to be made about the winner of a tied match or tournament, or the allocation of a match venue, the following rules apply.

National Provincial Championships

Round Robin Winner	
First option	Winner of round robin match
Second option	Higher differential of average points scored for and against throughout round robin

Semi-Finals	
First option	Extra 20 minutes playing time
Second option	Team scoring most tries during that match
Third option	Winner of round robin match
Fourth option	Higher differential of average points scored for and against throughout round robin

Finals	
All divisions	Declared joint winners

Super 12

Teams Tied (at completion of round robin series)	
First option	Margin of points scored for and against throughout the series
Second option	Winner of the pool match between those two teams
Third option	Team scoring most tries throughout the series

Semi-Finals	
First option	Extra 20 minutes playing time
Second option	Team scoring most tries
Third option	Team finishing highest in round robin series

Final Venue

Home ground of highest qualifying team successful in semi-final
(e.g., team 3 and team 4 win — final venue is team 3's home ground.)

Tournament Winner	
First option	Extra 20 minutes playing time
Second option	Declared joint winners

Tri-Nations

Tournament Winner	
First option	Ratio of points scored for and against throughout the series
Second option	Team scoring most tries throughout the series
Third option	Declared joint winners

Rugby World Cup

Pool Teams Tied (at completion of pool round)	
First option	Winner of the pool match between those two teams
Second option	Team scoring greatest number of points during pool round
Third option	Team scoring most tries in the match between the tied teams
Fourth option	Team scoring most tries throughout pool round
Fifth option	Ratio of points scored for and against throughout pool round
Sixth option	Team with least number of players ordered off throughout tournament
Seventh option	Toss of coin by team managers

Rugby World Cup (continued)

Knock-out Matches Tied	
First option	Extra 20 minutes playing time
Second option	Team scoring most tries during the match
Third option	Team with least number of players ordered off throughout tournament
Fourth option	Toss of coin by team managers

Tied Final Match	
First option	Extra 20 minutes playing time
Second option	Team scoring most tries during the match
Third option	Team with least number of players ordered off throughout tournament
Fourth option	Toss of coin by team managers